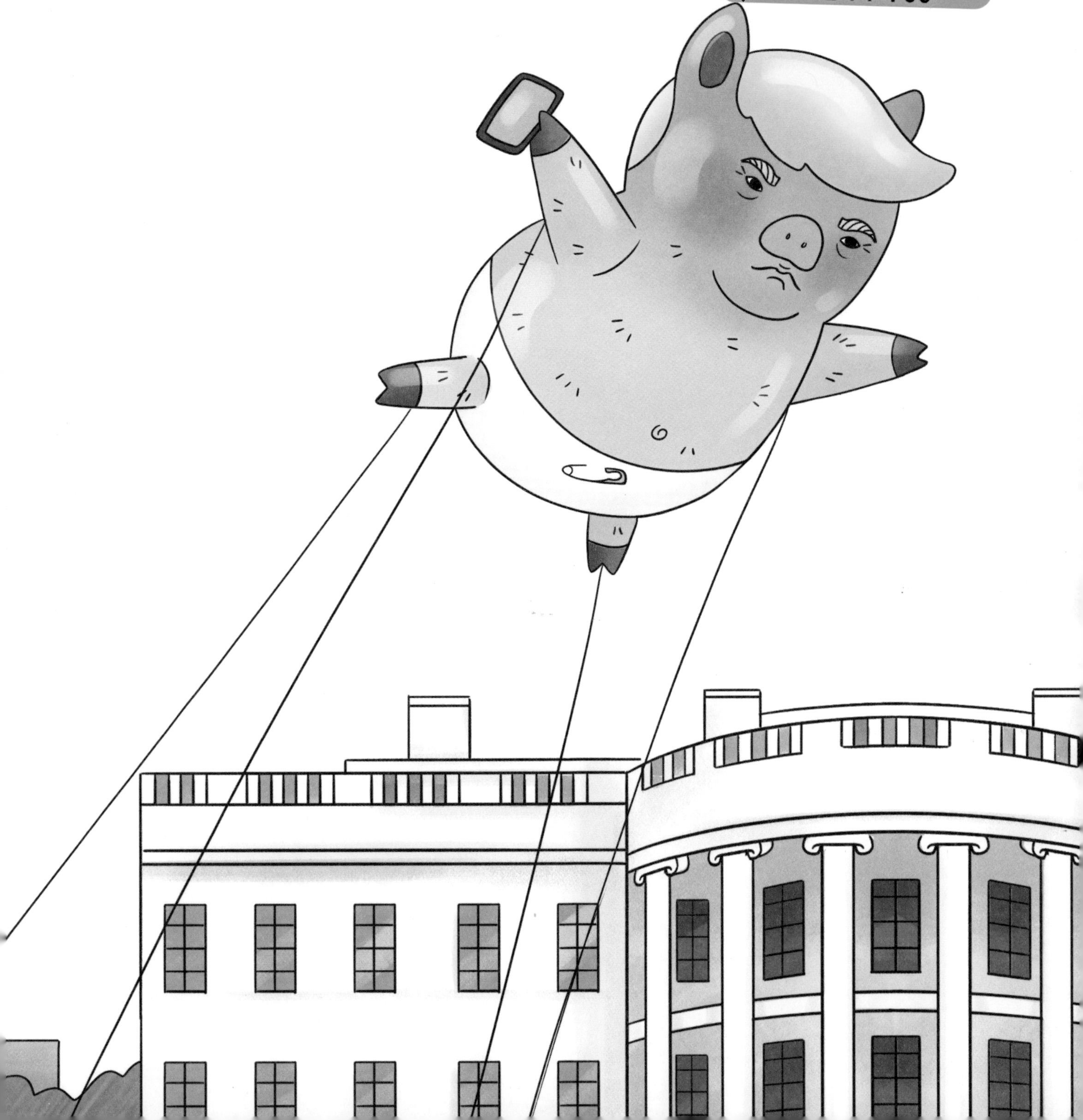

IF YOU GIVE
A PIG THE
WHITE HOUSE

A PARODY

www.castlepointbooks.com

The Castle Point Books trademark is
owned by Castle Point Publishing, LLC.
Castle Point books are published and
distributed by St. Martin's Press.

ISBN 978-1-250-25641-6 (hardcover)
ISBN 978-1-250-25642-3 (ebook)

Design by Katie Jennings Campbell
Illustrations by Amy Zhing

Our books may be purchased in bulk for promotional,
educational, or business use. Please contact your local
bookseller or the Macmillan Corporate and Premium Sales
Department at 1-800-221-7945, extension 5442,
or by email at MacmillanSpecialMarkets@macmillan.com.

First Edition: October 2019

10 9 8 7 6 5 4 3 2

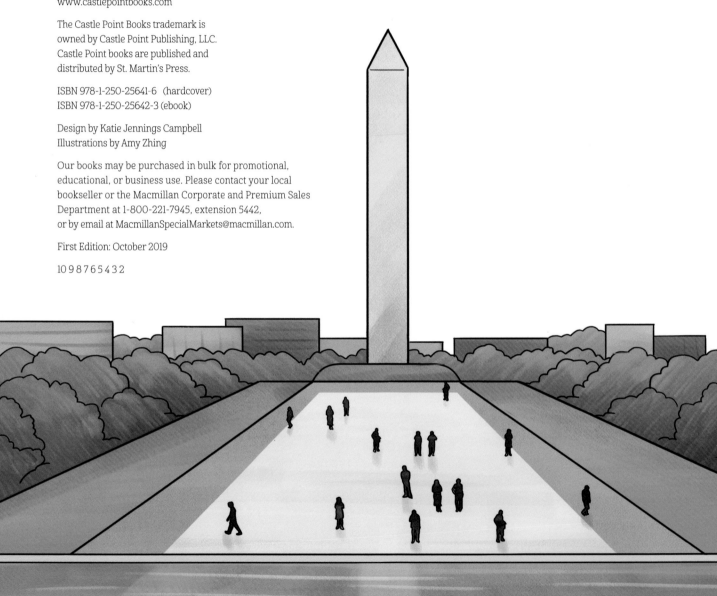

IF YOU GIVE A PIG THE WHITE HOUSE

BY FAYE KANOUSE

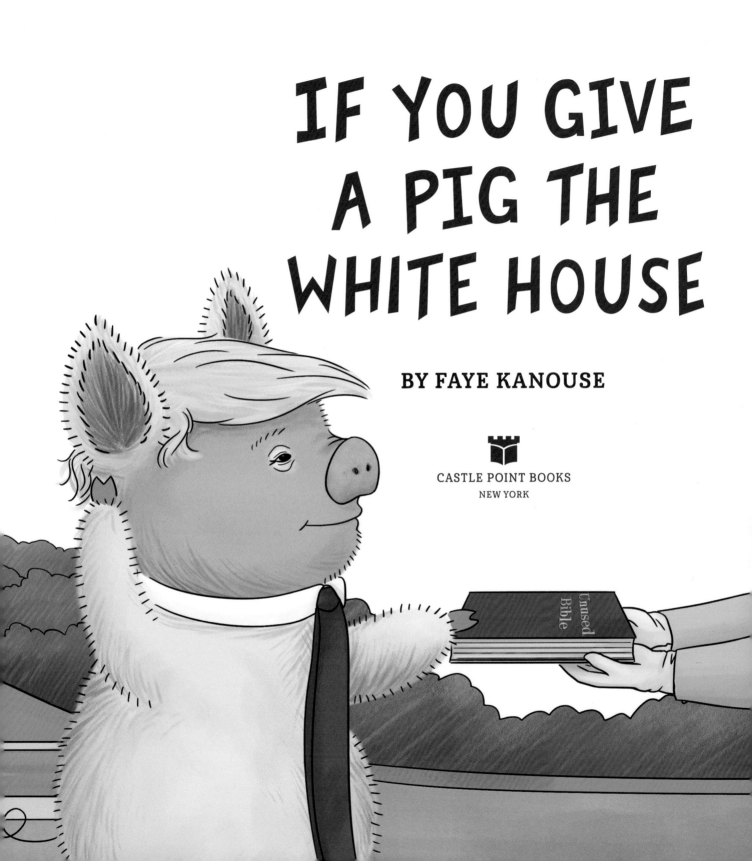

CASTLE POINT BOOKS

NEW YORK

If you give a pig
the White House,

he'll ask to
watch TV.

When you let him watch TV,
he'll want to tweet.

Tweeting will make him hungry, so you'll order his favorite meal.

When you serve him the well-done burgers, you'll have to make sure he gets more than everyone else.

Getting more than everyone else will remind him of his policy positions. So he'll ask you for a briefing.

When the briefing isn't brief enough,
his mind will probably start to wander.

When his mind wanders,
he will probably oversimplify
complex problems and make
unconstitutional decisions.

So you'll have to hire people with no integrity to help him get public support for his agenda.

When he speaks to the public,
he'll probably stumble over
big words, get mad, and lash out.

So you'll tell him to apologize. He won't like you telling him what to do, so he'll ramp up the insults and add in some lies.

When journalists ask about his lies, the pig will want to silence them by trampling on the First Amendment.

When his attempt at censorship
threatens American democracy,
you'll try to distract him.

You'll show him a solar eclipse.
He'll stare straight at it.

Then you'll take him to a doctor. This will remind him to destroy healthcare.

When that doesn't work, the pig will give diplomacy a try. He'll become an international laughingstock and buddy up to dictators.

When the dictators flatter him,
he'll want to do whatever they say.

So you'll have to bring him back to Washington. It will be cold when you land, so he'll declare that global warming is a hoax.

When climate change causes
another severe weather event,
you'll want him to look like he cares.

He'll soon get tired of pretending and want to blow off steam. That's when you'll probably hear some locker room talk.

You'll remind him that he has
work to do draining the swamp.

Mentioning the swamp will remind him that pigs love mud. He'll want you to make him a swamp all his own.

When he's satisfied with the swamp,
he'll ask for something even bigger.

He'll declare a national emergency just to get it.

After all this effort, he'll probably be tired.

So you'll have to pack
his bags for a golf trip.

When it starts to rain,
he'll want to tweet
and watch TV.
And chances are,
if he's tweeting
and watching TV...

He'll want the White House to do it in.